EXPLORING THE ELEMENTS

Mercury

Anita Louise McCormick

Enslow Publishing
101 W. 23rd Street
Suite 240
New York, NY 10011
USA
enslow.com

Published in 2019 by Enslow Publishing, LLC.
101 W. 23rd Street, Suite 240, New York, NY 10011

Library of Congress Cataloging-in-Publication Data

Names: McCormick, Anita Louise, author.
Title: Mercury / Anita Louise McCormick.
Description: New York : Enslow Publishing, [2019] | Series: Exploring the elements | Audience: Grades 5 to 8. | Includes bibliographical references and index.
Identifiers: LCCN 2018011251 | ISBN 9781978503670 (library bound) | ISBN 9781978505421 (paperback)
Subjects: LCSH: Mercury—Juvenile literature. | Periodic table of the elements—Juvenile literature.
Classification: LCC QD181.H6 M33 2018 | DDC 546/.663—dc23
LC record available at https://lccn.loc.gov/2018011251

Printed in the United States of America

To Our Readers: We have done our best to make sure all website addresses in this book were active and appropriate when we went to press. However, the author and the publisher have no control over and assume no liability for the material available on those websites or on any websites they may link to. Any comments or suggestions can be sent by email to customerservice@enslow.com.

Photo Credits: Cover, p. 1 (chemical element symbols) Jason Winter/Shutterstock .com; cover, p. 1 (mercury) Dr. Me/Shutterstock.com; p. 8 Ventin/Shutterstock.com; p. 10 o2 Photography/Alamy Stock Photo; p. 13 Panimoni/Shutterstock.com; p. 16 BlueRingMedia/Shutterstock.com; p. 19 LN.Vector pattern/Shutterstock.com; p. 21 Carlos Clarivan/Science Source; p. 23 lovemelovemypic/Shutterstock.com; p. 25 Yuangeng Zhang/Shutterstock.com; p. 27 dcwcreations/Shutterstock.com; p. 31 Robert and Jean Pollock/Science Source; p. 33 Album/Gus Regalado/Newscom; p. 37 Claxton/MCT/Newscom; p. 39 Powerphotos/Shutterstock.com; p. 40 Imaginechina/AP.

Contents

Introduction

The shiny liquid metal we know today as mercury has been used in one form or another since ancient times. But it was not always used as a pure element. In nature, mercury is most often found in a red-colored mineral, mercury sulfide (HgS), which is commonly known as cinnabar. For thousands of years, cinnabar was used for cave drawings and as a red pigment throughout much of human history. It was also used in some cosmetics and medicines—until scientists discovered just how toxic mercury exposure can be.

For hundreds of years, mercury was used by gold miners to separate gold from other materials. Since the mid-1600s, mercury has been used in scientific instruments, such as thermometers and barometers. During the electronic age, mercury was used for even more applications, such as mercury batteries, fluorescent lightbulbs, and silent wall switches. But while mercury's uses grew throughout the world, so did the problem of mercury pollution and poisoning.

At first, most people did not realize that exposure to mercury could make them ill. But as mines and chemical companies that used mercury sprang up, people started to notice that workers were becoming ill. The problem of mercury pollution was even more severe when waste water containing mercury was dumped into the water supply. That is what happened in Minamata, Japan, when a chemical factory, Chisso Corporation, dumped waste containing mercury into the bay. Aquatic life consumed mercury that was dumped into Minamata Bay. The shellfish in the bay, which were a major food supply, became contaminated with mercury. Soon, many people in the area became ill. The problem was first discovered in the late 1950s. In 2017, the Minamata Convention on Mercury put into effect laws that would help reduce mercury pollution in the environment and protect human health. The Minamata Convention is a global treaty. As of 2018, the document has been signed by 128 leaders and was ratified, or approved, by 89 countries.

Mercury is a cumulative poison, meaning that damage is done when it builds up in the body over time. It is also a neurotoxin, which can destroy nerve tissue, including the brain. Chronic, or long-term, mercury exposure can lead to tremors, extreme mood changes, hearing loss, and blindness. These factors make exposure to even small amounts of mercury extremely dangerous.

Even experts in handling dangerous chemicals can be accidentally poisoned by mercury and its compounds. In 1997, a Dartmouth

College chemistry professor and toxic metals specialist, Dr. Karen Wetterhahn, died at the age of forty-eight from mercury poisoning. She was accidentally poisoned when a few drops of a deadly compound of mercury, called dimethylmercury, came through the latex glove she was wearing. At the time, scientists believed that latex gloves offered sufficient protection, but later tests showed that dimethylmercury can seep through latex. Six months after the exposure, Dr. Wetterhahn started to show symptoms of mercury poisoning. She died nearly a year later. Now scientists know that the only safe way to handle dimethymercury is by wearing special heavy-duty gloves.

1

Mercury Is an Amazing Element

There are many amazing things about mercury. Out of all the elements, mercury is the only metal that exists as a liquid at room temperature. Only one other element, the nonmetallic element bromine (Br), remains a liquid under these conditions. "Element" is the scientific term for a substance that cannot be broken down into something simpler by using ordinary chemical means such as exposing it to acids, electricity, or heat.

Mercury Through the Ages

Mercury is a rare, naturally occurring element in Earth's crust. Mercury only makes up 0.08 parts per million of Earth's crust. Still, it was known to and used by the ancient Greeks, Romans, Chinese,

At room temperature, mercury is liquid and easily moves around in beautiful, reflective blobs.

and Hindus. Samples of the metal have been found in 3,500-year-old Egyptian tombs.

Mercury was also known to alchemists during the Middle Ages. The alchemists considered mercury, sulfur (S), and salt to be the three main substances that made up Earth. In fact, the Hindu word for "alchemy," *Rasasiddhi*, means “knowledge of mercury.” Alchemists believed that all metals were mixtures of mercury and other substances. At the time, alchemists knew of seven metals: mercury, gold (Au), silver (Ag), copper (Cu), tin (Sn), lead (Pb), and iron (Fe). They also believed that, given the right combination of ingredients, mercury could be transmuted, or changed, into gold. Unfortunately for the alchemists, one element cannot be changed into another element through ordinary chemical means. So, no matter how hard they tried, they were unsuccessful at turning mercury, or any other metal, into gold.

Mercury's toxic effects were also known to the ancients. They could see the illnesses suffered by miners who dug mercury compounds from the ground. These ailments started with tremors and progressed to full-blown mental derangement, or madness.

The saying "mad as a hatter" is also thought to have come from the use of a mercury compound, called mercury(II) nitrate, in the hat-making trade. This compound was used to make felt out of rabbit fur, and hats were manufactured with the felt. Workers in hat factories often suffered from serious health problems such as the loss of teeth and hair, memory loss, and the deterioration of their nervous systems. This general breakdown of nervous tissue, especially in the brain, may have caused mental derangement and bizarre behavior, causing people to coin the term "mad as a hatter." Because of the health risk of mercury exposure, the US Public Health Service banned the use of mercury(II) nitrate in the felt industry on December 1, 1941.

Mercury's chemical symbol is Hg. The "Hg" comes from the Greek word *hydrargyrum*. Hydrargyrum means "liquid silver." Because of its silvery appearance and the way it moves, the metal was also called quicksilver. In fact, the element is named for the Roman god Mercury, who was known for his speed and mobility. Mercury is also very heavy. It weighs 13.6 times the same volume of water.

Where Is Mercury Found?

Like most metals, mercury is rarely found in its pure state in nature. Most mercury that humans use comes from a mineral ore called cinnabar. The scientific name for cinnabar is mercury(II) sulfide (HgS).

A Fountain Where Mercury Flows

When the Spanish government approached Alexander Calder, an American sculptor and artist, to design a piece of art for the Spanish Pavilion at the 1937 World's Fair held in Paris, France, they asked him to design a fountain where mercury flowed instead of water. Calder designed the fountain to remind people of the capture of the Almadén mercury mines by General Francisco Franco during the Spanish Civil War (1936–1939). Calder's mercury fountain can still be seen at the Fundación Joan Miró in Barcelona, Spain. To prevent people from inhaling mercury vapor, though, it is now displayed behind glass.

This fountain, made for the 1937 World's Fair, contains mercury, not water.

Cinnabar is a bright red mineral, sometimes called vermillion. Because of its bright red color, vermillion was a popular pigment, or coloring. About twenty thousand years ago, ancient humans used cinnabar to make cave paintings. Scientists have also found prehistoric skulls painted with cinnabar in Italy. The pigment has also been discovered in Mayan ruins dating back to 500 BCE. Until recently, most cinnabar mining was done in Spain and Italy. Some mercury mines in Spain have been operating for more than two thousand years. Today, China and Kyrgyzstan are the world's top cinnabar mining countries.

Pure mercury can be obtained from cinnabar by heating the ore, in the presence of oxygen, to about 1100° F (590° C). The mercury in the rock turns to vapor, and the sulfur reacts with the oxygen to make sulfur dioxide. The mercury vapor is then cooled, causing it to condense into a liquid.

Mercury in the Environment

Mercury can be found nearly everywhere on Earth. Traces of mercury are naturally found in many rocks and other substances, including coal. When power plants burn coal that contains mercury to make electricity, mercury is released into the atmosphere. Coal-burning power plants are responsible for more than 40 percent of the human-caused mercury emissions in the United States. This makes coal-burning power plants one of the largest sources of mercury environmental contamination. This mercury in the air eventually settles onto the waters of oceans, lakes, and streams or onto land, where it can be washed into the water and converted into dangerous mercury compounds by microorganisms.

The Periodic Table

The periodic table is a chart that chemists use to organize the chemical elements based on the elements' properties. The rows on the periodic table are also called periods. Mercury is in period six. The columns on the periodic table are called groups or families. Mercury is found in group 12, or IIB (IIB is part of an old naming system), along with the elements zinc (Zn) and cadmium (Cd).

One of the first scientists to develop a periodic table was a Russian chemist named Dmitry Mendeleev (1834–1907). In Mendeleev's time, only about sixty elements were known. He arranged these elements in a chart in the order of their increasing atomic weights. Mendeleev left a few blank spaces in his chart, predicting that, one day, scientists would discover elements that would fill in the blanks. He even predicted what these properties would be. Within his lifetime, Mendeleev was proven correct with the discoveries of gallium (Ga) in 1875, scandium (Sc) in 1879, and germanium (Ge) in 1886. Since then, many other elements have been discovered. As of 2017, there are 118 known elements listed on the periodic table.

Elements have two different types of properties—physical and chemical. Physical properties of mercury include that it is a shiny liquid at room temperature. The metal is also heavy. If there were two identical cups, one that contained mercury and another that had the same volume of water in it, the cup with the mercury would weigh 13.6 times more than the one containing the water. The property responsible for the difference in weight is called density. Because mercury is so dense, pieces of iron and lead will float on its surface. Another of mercury's physical properties is that the metal

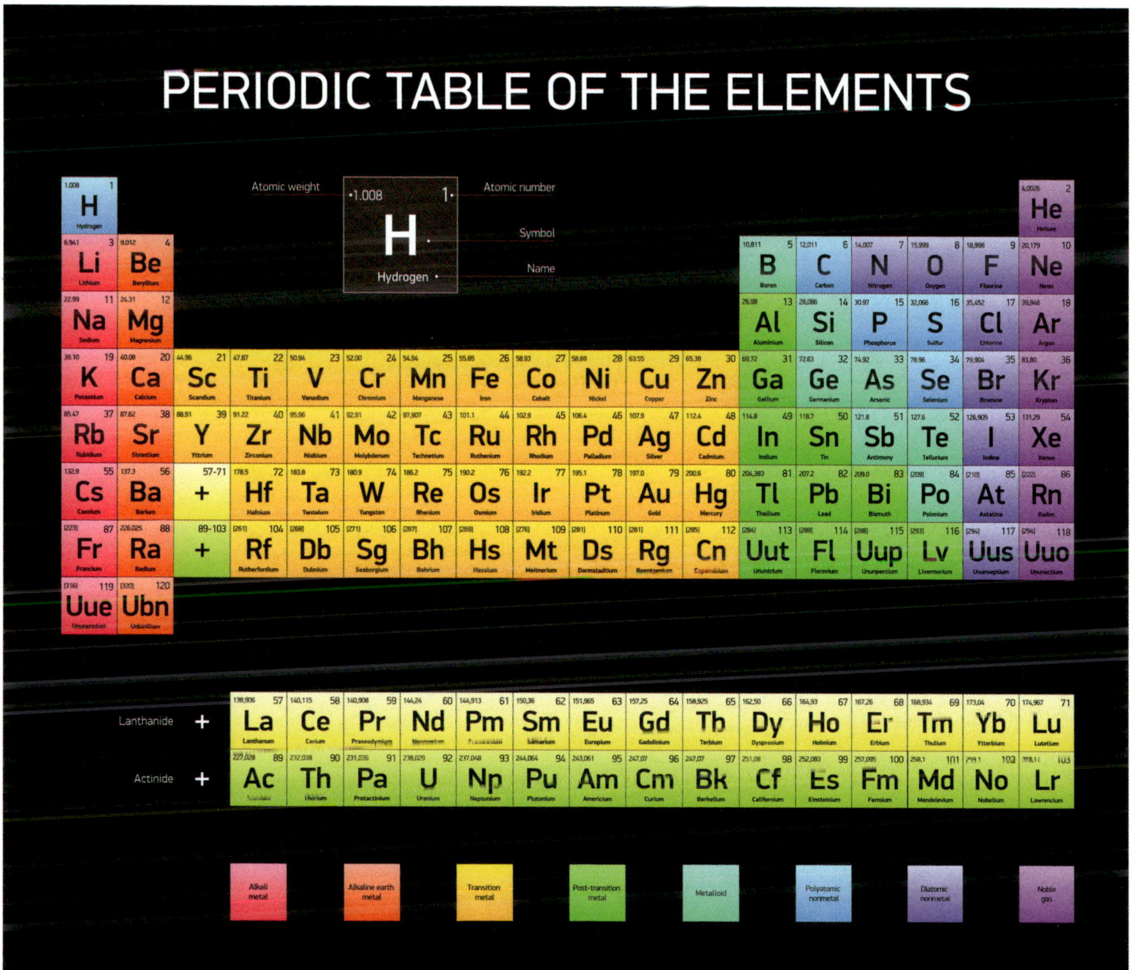

Mercury is the only metal that is liquid at room temperature, making it good to use in thermometers, barometers, and other measuring devices.

remains a liquid over a wide range of temperatures. Mercury freezes at -37.89° F (-38.83° C) and boils at 674.11° F (356.73° C).

Mercury has chemical properties, too. Chemical properties describe how the element reacts with other chemicals that come into contact with it. For example, mercury will chemically combine with nonmetallic elements such as sulfur, oxygen (O), and chlorine (Cl) to make chemical compounds. Chemical compounds form when two or more elements are chemically bonded together.

Mercury is classified as a transition metal. Metals are substances that are shiny, conduct heat and electricity well, and are malleable and ductile when solid. Most of the elements on the periodic table are metals. Mercury shares many properties of other metals, except it does not conduct heat well. The transition metals are represented in groups 3 through 12 (or IIIB–IIB) on the periodic table.

2

What Makes Up Mercury?

When Mendeleev came up with the idea of using a periodic table to list elements, only sixty elements were known. Today, scientists know of 118 elements. Mendeleev arranged his periodic table generally by the atomic weights of the elements. In 1913, however, Henry Moseley (1887–1915), a British physicist, discovered that an element's properties are determined more by its subatomic particles than by its weight.

Atoms—The Building Blocks of All Matter

All elements are made up of particles called atoms. Atoms are the building blocks of all matter. A car, the air, and even you are made up of atoms.

An element is a substance that contains only one type of atom. A sample of pure mercury, for example, is made up of many, many tiny mercury atoms. Atoms contain three subatomic particles—protons, neutrons, and electrons.

All mercury atoms contain eighty protons. If an atom does not contain eighty protons, it is not an atom of mercury, but it is an atom

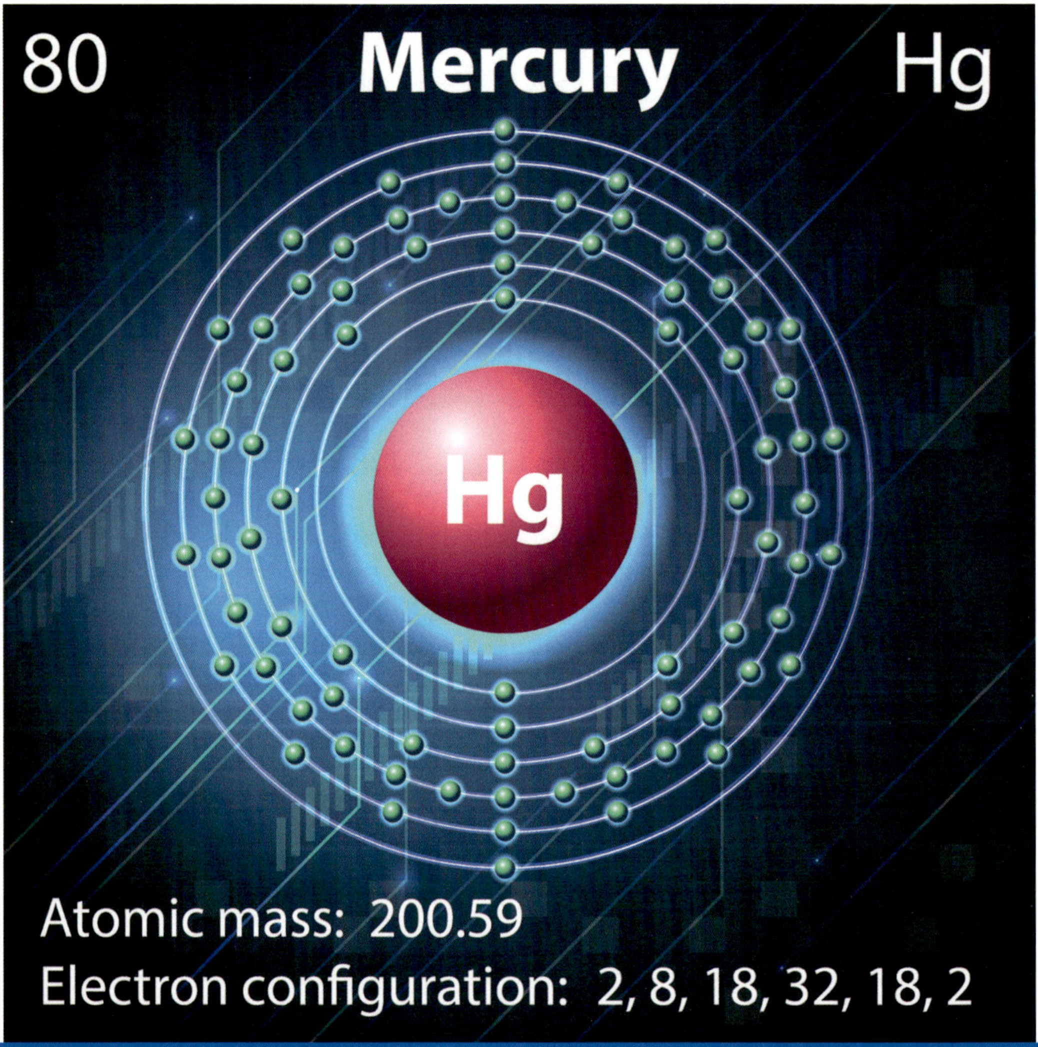

An atom of mercury, showing how the electrons fill the shells.

of some other element. An atom's atomic number is equal to its number of protons.

Mercury's atomic number is eighty. The elements on the modern periodic table are listed in order of increasing atomic number. Arranged in this way, the elements in the same groups, or columns, have similar properties. Protons are located in the nucleus, or center, of the atom. They have a positive charge and a weight of about 1.0 atomic mass unit (amu).

Neutrons are also found in the nucleus of an atom. Unlike protons, neutrons have no charge—they are neutral. But they do have mass; like protons, the weight of a neutron is about 1.0 amu. Together, the protons and neutrons make up the weight of an atom. On average, a mercury atom has 121 neutrons. Therefore, the average weight of a mercury atom is about 201 amu, 80 protons plus 121 neutrons.

The third type of subatomic particle, the electron, has such a small mass that its weight is not used to calculate the weight of an atom. However, electrons are very important subatomic particles. Because protons, which are positively charged, and neutrons, which have no charge, make up the nucleus of an atom, the nucleus has a net positive charge. Nevertheless, atoms are neutral. That means that the positive charge in an atom's nucleus must be balanced by an equal number of negatively charged particles. These negatively charged subatomic particles are electrons. Because mercury atoms have eighty protons, they must also have eighty electrons.

The electrons travel around outside the nucleus and are arranged in shells, or energy levels. The electrons on the highest energy level, or outermost shell, are called the valence electrons. These valence electrons are lost, gained, or shared with other elements during chemical reactions. This exchange of electrons is what forms chemical bonds between elements. When two or more elements are chemically bonded together, they form chemical compounds. Mercury has two valence electrons. When mercury chemically combines with oxygen, the mercury atom gives its two valence electrons to the oxygen atom. This creates a chemical bond between the mercury atom and the oxygen atom and forms a chemical compound called mercury(II) oxide (HgO).

Two Types of Mercury Ions

When metals chemically react with nonmetals, the metal loses some or all of its valence electrons, and the nonmetallic element takes the electrons in. When a metal loses electrons, it now has more protons in its nucleus than it has electrons. This gives the metal an overall positive charge. Because atoms are neutral, this charged particle is no longer called an atom—it is called an ion. The nonmetal atom that takes the electrons from mercury also forms an ion, a negative ion. The positive mercury ion and the negative nonmetal ion are attracted to each other by their opposite charges. This attraction forms a chemical bond, called an ionic bond because it involves ions.

Mercury is a transition metal. Transition metals often form more than one type of ion, and mercury is no exception. Sometimes a mercury atom will lose both of its valence electrons. When this happens, the ion has two more protons than it has electrons. That means that this type of ion has a charge of +2. Another type of ion can be formed when a mercury atom loses only one of its two valence electrons. This results in an ion that has a charge of +1.

Mercury at a Glance

Chemical Symbol: Hg
Classification: Transition metal
Properties: Silvery-white mirrorlike liquid; high density
Discovered By: Known since ancient times
Atomic Number: 80
Protons: 80
Electrons: 80
Neutrons: 121 (on average)
Atomic Weight: 200.59 atomic mass units (amu)
State of Matter at 68° Fahrenheit (20° Celsius): Liquid
Melting Point: -37.89° F (-38.83° C)
Boiling Point: 674.11° F (356.73° C)
Commonly Found: In Earth's crust, combined with the element sulfur in the mineral cinnabar (HgS) and the element chlorine in calomel (Hg_2Cl_2)

Mercury was once commonly known as hydrargyrum and retains its Hg abbreviation on the periodic table of elements.

Because there are two forms of mercury ions, chemists developed a way to name mercury-containing chemical compounds that will show which type of ion is in the compound. To do this, they use a Roman numeral in the compound's name. The Roman numeral shows which type of ion is in the compound. When mercury combines with oxygen, for example, two different compounds can be formed—mercury(I) oxide (Hg_2O) and mercury(II) oxide (HgO). Mercury(I) oxide contains the ion that has a +1 charge. Mercury(II) oxide has the ion that has lost both valence electrons and has a charge of +2.

Mercury's Isotopes

The atomic weight of atoms is not always the same. Mercury's atomic weight is often listed on periodic tables as 201 amu. But that is not always the case. Even though all mercury atoms have the same number of protons, they do not all have the same number of neutrons. Forms of an element that have different numbers of neutrons than standard atoms of that element are called isotopes. The atomic weight of mercury, as well as other elements, that is listed on the periodic table takes into account all that element's isotopes and in what proportion they are found.

There are seven naturally occurring isotopes of mercury. The most common mercury isotope is mercury-202. The number that appears after the element's name is its weight. Because all atoms of mercury have eighty protons, and the number of protons plus the number of neutrons adds up to an atom's weight, this isotope must have 122 neutrons. Almost 30 percent of all mercury atoms are mercury-202.

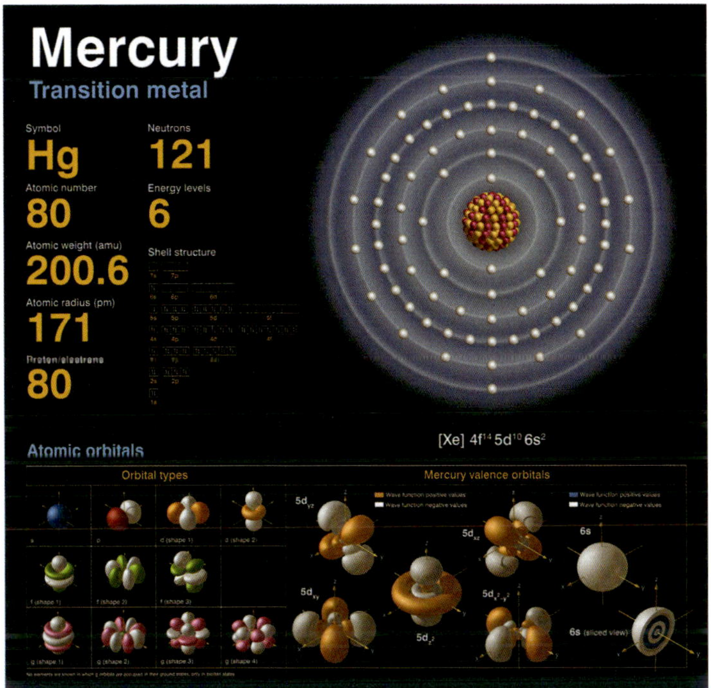

Mercury is a transition metal, along with copper, iron, nickel, and zinc.

The heaviest mercury isotope is mercury-204. Mercury-204 contains 124 neutrons and makes up about 7 percent of mercury atoms. The lightest and rarest mercury isotope is mercury-196. Less than 1 percent of all mercury atoms are mercury-196.

The other four mercury isotopes are mercury-198, mercury-199, mercury-200, and mercury-201. Taking into account the masses and percents of the isotopes, the average weight of a mercury atom is 200.59 amu, the atomic weight that is listed on some periodic tables. This type of average is called a weighted average. On other periodic tables, such as the one in this book, mercury's atomic weight is rounded to the nearest whole number (201 amu).

3

Uses for Mercury in Modern Electronics

Mercury is toxic to humans. However, when it is handled safely, mercury is a very useful element. For many years, mercury has been used in scientific instruments and household products such as thermometers, barometers, thermostats, silent wall switches, and fluorescent lightbulbs. In recent years, mercury use in devices used in homes, businesses, and scientific laboratories has decreased due to safety concerns.

Mercury in Thermometers

The first sealed liquid-in-glass thermometer was invented by Ferdinand II (1610–1670), the Grand Duke of Tuscany, in 1654. His thermometer was filled with alcohol and was not very accurate. In 1714, Gabriel Fahrenheit (1686–1736), a German physicist, improved the accuracy of the thermometer by replacing alcohol with mercury. Fahrenheit also developed a standardized temperature scale that is still in use in the United States.

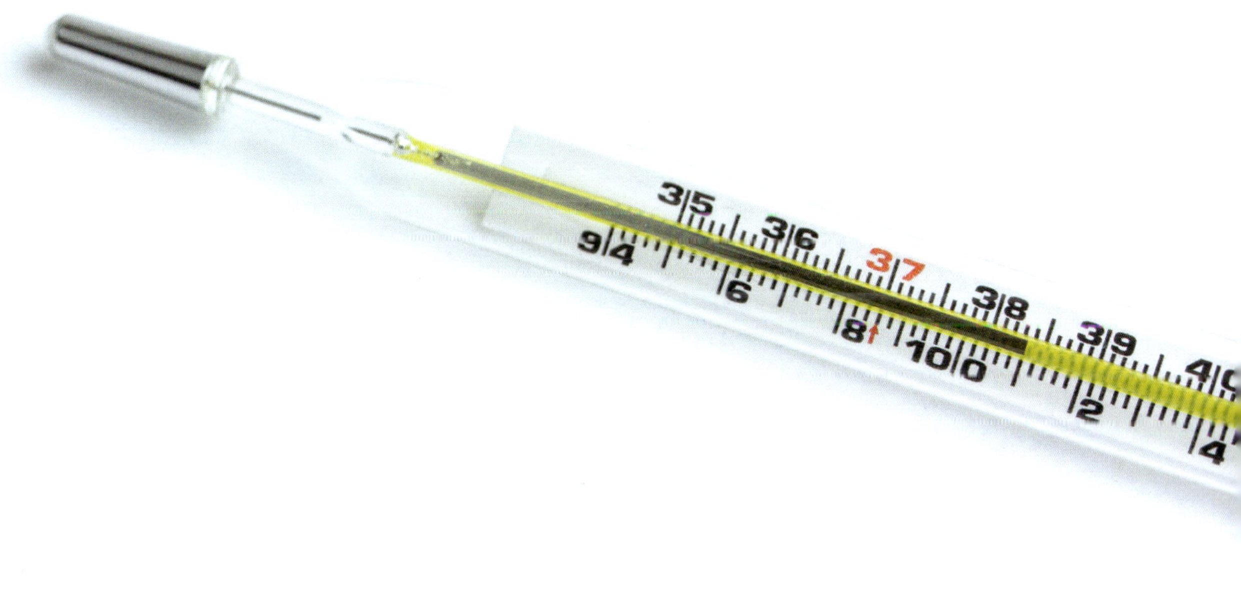

When heated, mercury moves, which makes it ideal to use in thermometers.

Almost all liquids expand, or get bigger, when the temperature increases. The liquid inside a liquid-in-glass thermometer is held in a bulb at the bottom. The bulb is attached to a narrow tube at its top. When the liquid expands, there is nowhere for it to go but up into the tube, making the liquid move higher on the temperature scale. In addition, most liquids (with the notable exception of water) contract, or get smaller, when the temperature goes down. As the liquid contracts, it moves down the temperature scale, registering a lower temperature.

Mercury thermometers are slightly more accurate than those filled with alcohol. If a mercury thermometer is broken, however, it can expose people to toxic mercury vapor. Because of these health concerns, many scientific laboratories and households are willing to sacrifice a little bit of accuracy in favor of safety. A red dye is often added to the alcohol to make it easier to see movement up and down the temperature scale.

Mercury is also used in barometers (instruments that measure atmospheric pressure) and other scientific equipment. This can pose a health risk to chemists working in laboratories where these instruments are used. If a thermometer, barometer, or other piece of equipment is broken, for example, the mercury can quickly fill cracks on lab benches and floors. That makes it very hard to clean up. Mercury that is not properly disposed of can easily vaporize, endangering the safety of laboratory workers or anyone else that comes in contact with it.

Mercury's Use in Switches

Like most other metals, mercury conducts electricity. Because of this property, mercury has been used in electrical switches and thermostats. Mercury light switches look just like regular light switches, but they do not "click" like other types of light switches do when you flip them on. For this reason, these switches are sometimes called silent switches. Mercury light switches were made and sold from the late 1960s until 1991. They can still be found in some older homes and businesses.

Mercury in Arctic Permafrost

Harmful greenhouse gases trapped in the Arctic permafrost are being released due to global warming. In early 2018, a team of scientists with the US Geological Survey announced that as the Arctic permafrost melts with rising temperatures, mercury gas trapped there will also be released. According to its article in *Geophysical Research Letters*, approximately 32 million gallons of mercury is currently trapped in the Arctic permafrost. That is enough to fill fifty Olympic-size swimming pools! When mercury is released from permafrost, it goes into the air, soil, and water. The amount of mercury released will depend on how much of the permafrost melts.

As the world's climate changes, Arctic permafrost is thawing; as this ground thaws, it will release stored gases and other elements, including mercury.

When the light switch is flipped, the mercury moves to surround electrical contacts inside the switch. This action completes an electrical circuit, allowing electricity to flow through the wires and turn the light on. When the light switch is turned off, the mercury moves away from the electrical contacts. This movement breaks the circuit and turns the light out.

A thermostat is the device that monitors and controls furnaces and air conditioners. Many thermostats contain mercury tilt switches. The mercury in these switches is enclosed in a small glass capsule. Inside the capsule, there are electrical contacts at one end. When the switch is tilted, the mercury collects at the end with the contacts, where it completes a circuit that allows electricity to flow through. When the mercury goes to the other end, the circuit is broken.

If silent wall switches and thermostats are in good working condition, there is virtually no health risk from the mercury switches. If they are removed, they should be brought to a household hazardous waste collection center, not tossed into the trash.

Mercury in Fluorescent Lightbulbs

Mercury is also used in some lightbulbs. Fluorescent lightbulbs are filled with a small amount of mercury vapor and argon (Ar) gas. When electricity is passed through the bulb, electrons in the mercury atoms absorb enough energy to move them to a higher energy level. This is called the excited state. When the electrons fall back to their regular energy level, their ground state, they give off radiation, some of which is ultraviolet (UV). However, humans cannot see UV radiation. To convert UV to visible light, the insides of fluorescent lightbulbs are coated with a chemical powder called a phosphor. When the phosphor is hit by UV, the phosphor's electrons are excited to a higher energy level, too. When those electrons fall back to their ground state, they emit visible light.

Compact fluorescent lightbulbs, known as CFL bulbs, also contain mercury vapor. They were widely sold for home and business use in the past two decades because of their energy savings over

In a mercury switch, the mercury is liquid and moves freely, completing an electrical circuit, which conducts electricity to turn a light on.

incandescent bulbs. As prices for mercury-free LED (light emitting diode) lightbulbs come down, many homes and businesses concerned about energy cost have switched to them.

Mercury Amalgams

One unusual characteristic of mercury is that it will dissolve other metals. When other metals are dissolved in mercury, they form a special type of alloy called an amalgam. Alloys are mixtures of two or more elements, at least one of which is a metal. Alloys are used because their properties are different from the elements they are made up of. Mercury alloys are called amalgams. Amalgams can be liquid or solid.

Dental amalgams are used by dentists to make fillings for cavities. They are made by dissolving silver dust in mercury. When a silver-mercury dental amalgam is first mixed, it is a liquid. As it cools and hardens, the amalgam expands to fill the hole where the cavity formed in the tooth.

Gold will also dissolve in mercury. As a result, mercury is often used to extract gold from its ore. The gold-mercury amalgam is heated, allowing the mercury to vaporize, leaving pure gold behind. When the mercury vapor is cooled, it condenses back into a liquid and can be used again.

4

Mercury's Use in Compounds

Mercury is a useful element on its own. But when mixed with other elements to create compounds, mercury has even more applications. Chemical compounds are formed when two or more elements are chemically bonded together. These compounds have unique properties of their own.

Mercury and compounds that contain mercury can be toxic. Sodium (Na), iron, and zinc are essential for the human body to work properly, but mercury has no beneficial purpose in the human body. Once inside the body, mercury and its compounds chemically react with enzymes. Enzymes are proteins that are essential for the body to function properly. When mercury reacts with the body's enzymes, it chemically changes the enzymes, and they can no longer do the job they normally do. This causes the health problems associated with mercury poisoning.

Poisons Made with Mercury

The same properties that make mercury poisonous to humans also make it poisonous to insects, fungi, and bacteria. Mercury(II) chloride ($HgCl_2$) is a poisonous salt. It is also soluble, meaning it can be dissolved in water. It was once used as a fungicide, a chemical substance that destroys fungus, and as a pesticide, a chemical substance that kills rodents, such as rats. In the past, it has also been used to keep wood from rotting as well as to disinfect surfaces and wounds. Because the compound is so poisonous, scientists have tried to find other chemicals to take the place of mercury(II) chloride.

Mercury(II) chloride is not the only poisonous salt of mercury. Mercury(I) chloride (Hg_2Cl_2) is toxic, too. Mercury(I) chloride does not dissolve in water as easily as mercury(II) chloride does, so it is not as dangerous. Mercury(I) chloride is also called calomel, once used as an antiseptic. Antiseptics slow the growth of bacteria. Doctors formerly prescribed the compound as an internal medicine, too. It was given because it works as a strong laxative, and it was used to treat syphilis, a sexually transmitted disease. Calomel was also a common ingredient in teething powers, which were used to numb the sore gums of teething babies, until the dangers of the

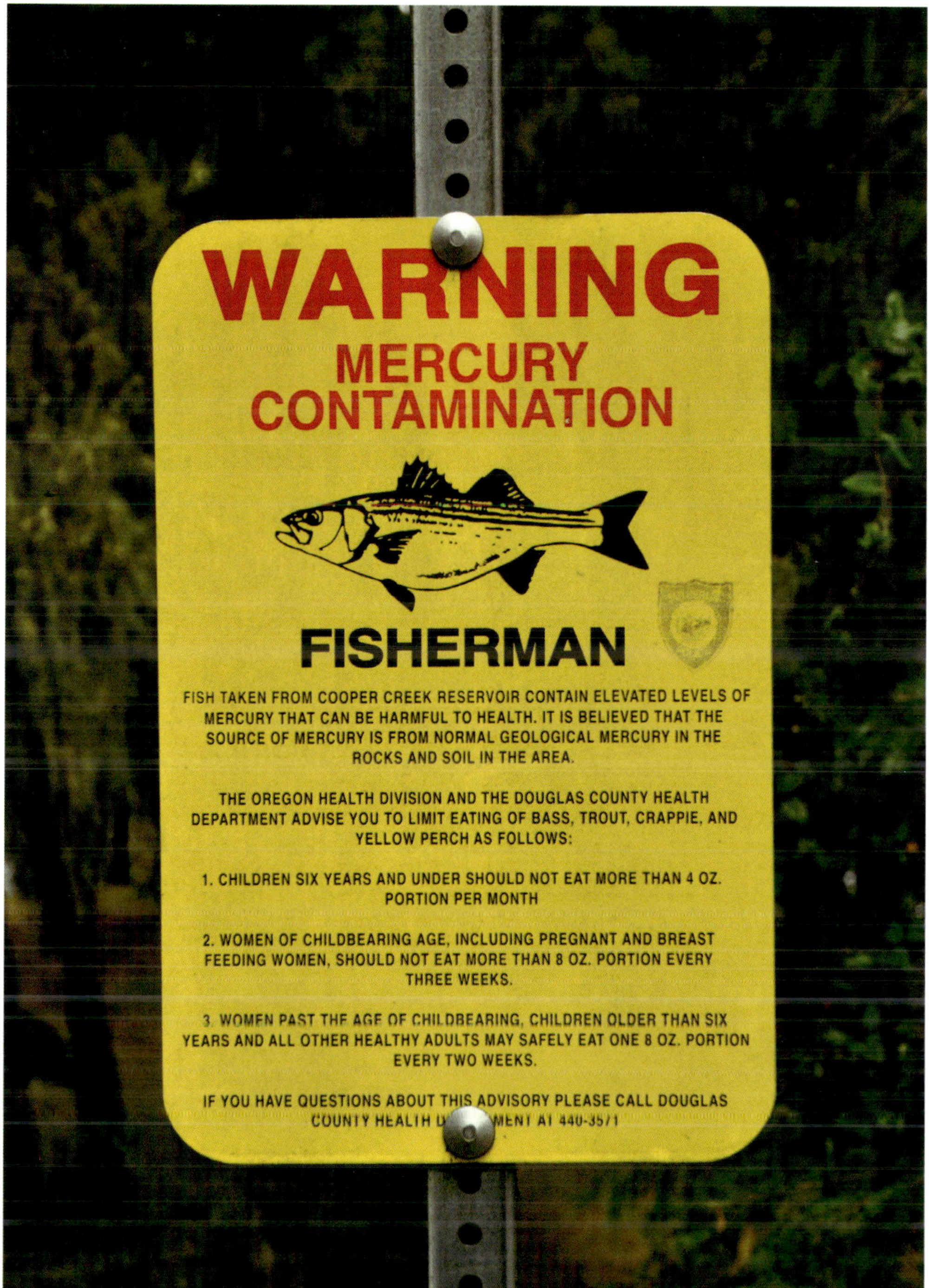

Mercury is poisonous to humans, fish, insects, fungi, and bacteria. Mercury often contaminates rivers and lakes, leading to fish contamination.

compound were discovered and publicized in 1948. Today, calomel is sometimes employed in agriculture to control root maggots and other pests on underground plant parts, such as tubers, roots, and bulbs.

Mercury Is Used to Make Explosives

Another mercury compound, mercury(II) fulminate [Hg(ONC)2], is dangerous in another way. It is highly explosive and used to make blasting caps. The explosive is very sensitive to friction (rubbing) and shock (striking). In an episode of the television show *Breaking Bad*, a drug dealer's office is blown up with a crystal of mercury fulminate; *Mythbusters*' Aaron Paul and Adam Savage proved the amount of mercury fulminate used on the show (50g) wouldn't have blown anything sky high. It took a whopping 250g to destroy the entire room.

Mercury fulminate was used to make blasting caps, but it takes rather a large amount to explode.

Mercury Batteries Power Electronic Devices

Mercury(II) chloride is not the only mercury compound that has been used in batteries. Mercury(II) oxide (HgO) was also once used as the positive electrode, or cathode, in dry cell batteries such as those found in radios, flashlights, and portable CD players.

The negative electrode, or the anode, of these batteries is usually made of zinc. The advantage of a mercury battery over other batteries is that it can supply a constant voltage, even when it gets old and the battery is partially drained. The disadvantage is that its mercury is highly toxic and needs to be properly disposed of.

Because many people did not take proper care and just tossed these batteries in their household trash, however, mercury batteries have been banned in the United States since the 1980s. Mercury batteries are still sold in some parts of Europe and Asia.

Mercury in Organic Compounds

All the mercury compounds discussed so far are inorganic compounds. Inorganic compounds are compounds that are not derived from living organisms. Scientists have found that some microorganisms (microscopic organisms that are too small to be seen with the human eye) can convert mercury into an organic compound. Organic

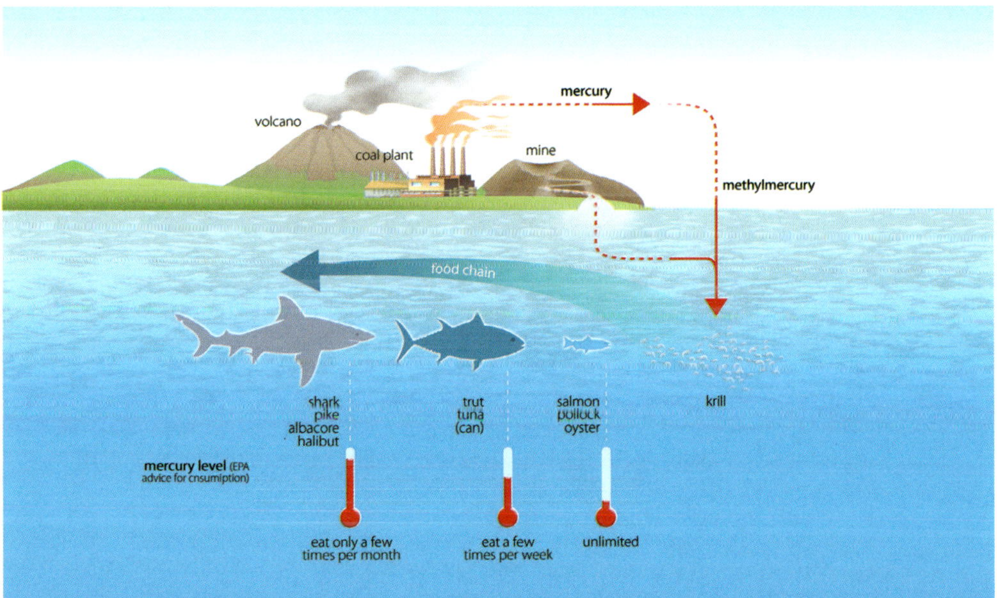

Mercury can contaminate water in a number of ways, but each one results in contaminated fish, which are unhealthy for people to consume.

compounds are compounds that contain the element carbon. They often have the elements hydrogen (H) and oxygen (O) in them, too.

The microorganisms that the scientists found live in lakes, streams, and rivers. When it rains, mercury-containing compounds run off the land and into the water. Additional mercury enters the water through the emissions of coal-burning power plants and waste incinerators. Once the mercury is in the water, the microorganisms absorb the mercury. Then they chemically change the mercury into an organic compound called methylmercury.

Small fish eat the microorganisms that contain the methylmercury, and the compound builds up in the fish's tissues. Larger fish eat the smaller fish, and more and more mercury accumulates in the food chain. This accumulation is called biomagnification. Humans who eventually eat the fish get a fairly high dose of methylmercury from them.

Unfortunately, the organic form of mercury is much more dangerous to humans than the inorganic mercury. Inside the human body, methylmercury can cause neurological and brain damage. In pregnant women, too much methylmercury can lead to birth defects in the baby. Because of the risk of mercury poisoning, governments and scientists are working to reduce the amount of mercury-containing substances that find their way into the water supply.

5

The Dangers of Mercury Poisoning

Mercury can enter the body in many ways. It can enter through the lungs, the digestive tract, or the skin. The amount of mercury that will be absorbed depends on how the element gets into the body. Because the lungs are very efficient at absorbing mercury vapor, it is much more dangerous to humans than liquid mercury.

Soluble mercury compounds are also dangerous because they are easily absorbed by the body. Small amounts of mercury can be eliminated by the body without doing much harm because the kidneys produce a protein that binds tightly with mercury atoms. Limited exposure to small amounts of metallic mercury and insoluble mercury compounds does not have the same effect on the body as vaporized mercury, soluble mercury compounds, and organic mercury compounds.

Mercury Poisoning from Eating Fish

Officials at the US Environmental Protection Agency (EPA) and the Food and Drug Administration (FDA) are very concerned about the possible health effects caused by eating fish contaminated with methylmercury. For this reason, the EPA and FDA work together to provide the public with guidelines about which species of fish should be avoided.

The first documented case of methylmercury poisoning occurred in Japan in 1958. Japanese fishermen and their families who lived in the area around Minamata Bay on the Japanese island of Kyushu started to get sick. During that time, sixty-eight people died and almost four hundred others exhibited some level of neurological damage. Scientists later found that industries around the bay were discharging elemental mercury into the bay. Bacteria living in the bay turned the metallic mercury into methylmercury. The fishermen and their families got sick because they ate a lot of fish caught in the bay.

Methylmercury affects the central nervous system and can cause paralysis, "tunnel vision," and blindness. A baby exposed to methylmercury in the womb may be born with neurological damage resembling cerebral palsy, if it survives at all. (Cerebral palsy is a disability resulting from damage to the brain at or before birth that can

A guide to eating healthy fish

Some species with high omega-3 fatty acids and relatively low levels of mercury (3.5 ounces of fish)

Fish	Omega-3 fatty acids (milligrams)	Mercury*
Farmed salmon	2,648	<0.05
Wild salmon	1,043	<0.05
Sardines	982	<0.05
Trout	935	0.07
Shrimp	315	<0.05
Some species with higher levels of contamination		
Tilefish	905	1.45
Swordfish	819	0.98
Shark	689	0.99
King mackerel	401	0.73
Some species that are a mixed bag		
Albacore tuna	862	0.35
Light tuna	270	0.12

*Mercury is a toxic metal; it's measured in parts per million.
The FDA has previously issued warnings for mercury levels over 0.35.

Source: Journal of the American Medical Association
Graphic: Chicago Tribune

Some fish are safer to eat than others when it comes to potential mercury levels.

cause muscular incoordination and speech problems.) For this reason, the EPA and FDA recommend that pregnant women avoid fish that may be contaminated with methylmercury.

Yet, eating fish can be an important part of a healthy diet. Scientific studies have shown that eating fish can lead to a lower likelihood of developing heart disease. Fish are low in fat and high in protein and omega-3 fatty acids. The trick is to eat enough heart-healthy fish without being exposed to too much mercury. For most people, the risk of eating fish or shellfish contaminated with mercury is not much of a health concern. In spite of this, for some people, such as women who are pregnant or hoping to get pregnant, nursing mothers, and young children, fish with high levels of methylmercury should be avoided.

Large fish at the top of the food chain such as shark, swordfish, or king mackerel are much more likely to contain high levels of methylmercury. Therefore, shrimp, canned light tuna, salmon, pollock, and catfish are better choices for pregnant women and young children because they contain lower methylmercury levels. The FDA and the EPA recommend eating up to 12 ounces, or two average meals, that contain these fish per week. Albacore tuna, another popular type of canned "white" tuna, contains more methylmercury than other types of canned light tuna. For this reason, the FDA and the EPA recommend eating no more than 6 ounces (one average meal) of albacore tuna per week.

Other Ways Mercury Poisoning Can Happen

Eating fish is not the only way people can be exposed to mercury. In 1971–1972, more than 6,500 Iraqis fell ill and almost 500 died when several countries responded to a famine by shipping packages of wheat grain intended for planting to Iraq. The wheat grains had been treated with a fungicide to keep mold from growing on the grain, but the fungicide contained methylmercury. The seeds were colored with a red dye to warn people of the danger of eating the seeds directly, but the warnings on the seed bags were not printed in a language understood by the Iraqis. Many Iraqi families ground the wheat grains into flour and used this flour to make bread. When they ate the bread baked with the contaminated flour, they became ill. The use of methylmercury as a fungicide is now banned in the United States, and because fungicide was the only commercial use for the compound, it is no longer made.

Mercury's Use in Vaccines

Thimerosal, a mercury-containing preservative, has been used in vaccines since the 1930s. In 1999, the American Academy of Pediatrics and the Public Health Service recommended that thimerosal in vaccines be reduced or eliminated, and today, with the exception of some flu shots, none of the childhood vaccines administered in the United States contain thimerosal.

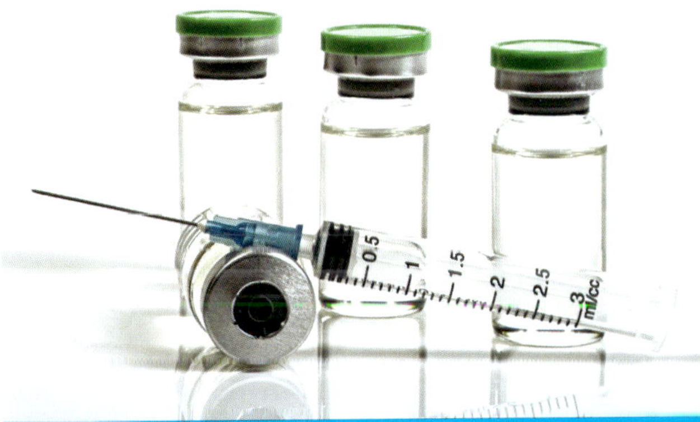

Thimerosal, a mercury-containing preservative, has been removed from most childhood vaccines.

Seeds and grains can easily be contaminated by mercury-rich waters; this mercury can then be digested when people eat the grains.

People who use mercury thermometers in their homes are normally not in danger of being poisoned by it. But whenever mercury is present, there is always a risk. This is especially true of people that deal with mercury in their workplace. During the 1970s and 1980s workers at a mercury thermometer plant in Vermont started to notice they were experiencing a common set of heath problems.

When the workers were tested, mercury was found in their bodies. Mercury vapor was also found in the air in the workers' homes and on their clothing and furniture. Their children also tested positive for mercury exposure. This incident was a first. Never before had parents' exposure to mercury been known to affect their children. The plant closed in 1984.

Due to the risk of mercury poisoning, and the fact that mercury is an element and cannot be broken down, people must be very careful how they handle and dispose of objects that contain mercury. While the use of mercury in batteries and thermometers has decreased in recent years, products containing mercury are still in use. Always take items you suspect might contain mercury to a hazardous waste disposal site instead of throwing them in your household trash. Taking these precautions will help keep mercury out of landfills, water supplies, and humans.

Glossary

alloy A mixture of two or more elements, at least one of which is a metal.

amalgam An alloy of mercury.

atom The smallest particle of matter.

compound A substance that contains two or more elements chemically bonded together.

density The weight per unit volume of a substance.

ductile Describes a physical property most metals have that allows them to be drawn into wires.

electron A negatively charged subatomic particle that moves around an atom's nucleus.

element A substance that cannot be broken down into a simpler substance through ordinary chemical means.

excited state A state in which an atom has absorbed enough energy to move an electron from a lower energy level to a higher one.

ion A charged particle that is formed when valence electrons are lost or gained.

isotopes Atoms of the same element that have a different number of neutrons.

malleable Describes a physical property of most metals that allows them to be hammered or rolled into sheets.

matter Anything that has mass and takes up space.

neurotoxin A substance that can damage nervous tissue.

neutron A neutral subatomic particle found in the nucleus of an atom.

nucleus The tiny center of an atom, which contains nearly all of its mass.

organic compound A chemical compound that contains carbon.

proton A positively charged subatomic particle that is found in the nucleus of an atom.

valence electrons Electrons in an atom's outermost shell, in the highest energy level.

Further Reading

Books

Baby Professor. *How Is Mercury Used Today?* Newark, DE: Speedy Publishing, LLC., 2017.

Callery, Sean, and Miranda Smith. *The Periodic Table*. New York, NY: Scholastic Nonfiction, 2017.

Csiszar, John. *Aluminum—Chemistry of Everyday Elements*, Broomdale, PA: Mason Crest, 2017.

DK. *The Elements Book: A Visual Encyclopedia of the Periodic Table*. New York, NY: DK Children, 2017.

Websites

Chemistry Explained

www.chemistryexplained.com/elements/L-P/Mercury.html

Facts and properties about mercury.

Live Science

www.livescience.com/39232-facts-about-mercury.html

The latest news and uses of mercury!

ThoughtCo.

www.thoughtco.com/mercury-element-facts-608433

Photographs and articles about mercury and how we use it every day.

Bibliography

Alden, Andrew. "About Mercury: The Geology of Quicksilver." ThoughtCo Lifelong Learning, March 17, 2017. https://www.thoughtco.com/all-about-mercury-1440918.

Blanc, Paul. *How Everyday Products Make People Sick: Toxins at Home and in the Workplace*. Berkeley, CA: University of California Press, 2007.

Centers for Disease Control and Prevention. "Thimerosal in Vaccines." Retrieved March 1, 2018. https://www.cdc.gov/vaccinesafety/concerns/thimerosal/index.html.

Chan, Anna. "'MythBusters' Proves 'Breaking Bad's' Walt needs some More Schooling." *The Today Show*, August 2013. https://www.today.com/popculture/mythbusters-proves-breaking-bads-walt-needs-some-more-schooling-6C10904583.

Chemistry Explained. "Mercury." Retrieved March 2, 2018. http://www.chemistryexplained.com/elements/L-P/Mercury.html

Cobb, Cathy, and Harold Goldwhite. *Creations of Fire: Chemistry's Lively History from Alchemy to the Atomic Age*. New York, NY: Plenum Press, 1995.

Helmenstine, Anne Marie. "How to Dispose of Mercury." ThoughtCo. Lifelong Learning, July 12, 2017. https://www.thoughtco.com/how-to-dispose-of-mercury-608447 Retrieved March 2, 2018.

Jefferson Lab. "It's Elemental—the Element Mercury." Retrieved March 1, 2018. http://education.jlab.org/itselemental/ele080.html.

Larson, Nina. "Groundbreaking Mercury Treaty Adopted By 140 Countries." *Business Insider*, Agence France Press. Retrieved March 5, 2018.http://www.businessinsider.com/groundbreaking-mercury-treaty-adopted-by-140-countries-2013-1.

Mooney, Chris. "The Arctic Is Full of Toxic Mercury, and Climate Change Is Going to Release It." *Washington Post*, February 5, 2018. https://www.washingtonpost.com/news/energy-environment/wp/2018/02/05/the-arctic-is-full-of-toxic-mercury-and-climate-change-is-going-to-release-it/?utm_term=.f8f53e7071df.

Rowlatt, Justin. "Mercury: A Beautiful but Poisonous Metal." BBC.com, November 30, 2013. http://www.bbc.com/news/magazine-25130770.

Royal Society of Chemistry, "Mercury." Retrieved March 2, 2018. http://www.rsc.org/periodic-table/element/80/mercury.

S. Brannan and Sons, Ltd. "Who Invented the Thermometer?" Retrieved March 2, 2018. http://www.brannan.co.uk/thermometers/invention.html.

Stwertka, Albert. *A Guide to the Elements*. New York, NY: Oxford University Press, 2002.

US Environmental Protection Agency. "Advisories and Technical Resources for Fish and Shellfish Consumption." Retrieved March 1, 2018. http://www.epa.gov/waterscience/fishadvice/advice.html.

US Environmental Protection Agency. "Health Effects of Exposures to Mercury." Retrieved March 2, 2018. https://www.epa.gov/mercury/health-effects-exposures-mercury.

US Environmental Protection Agency. "Mercury in Your Environment." Retrieved March 1, 2018. http://www.epa.gov/mercury/about.htm.

World Health Organization. "Mercury and Health." 2017. http://www.who.int/mediacentre/factsheets/fs361/en/.